A Holiday Swap

by Lana Cruce

illustrated by Diana Kizlauskas

Scott Foresman
is an imprint of

PEARSON

Glenview, Illinois • Boston, Massachusetts • Mesa, Arizona
Shoreview, Minnesota • Upper Saddle River, New Jersey

Every effort has been made to secure permission and provide appropriate credit for photographic material. The publisher deeply regrets any omission and pledges to correct errors called to its attention in subsequent editions.

Unless otherwise acknowledged, all photographs are the property of Pearson.

Photo locations denoted as follows: Top (T), Center (C), Bottom (B), Left (L), Right (R), Background (Bkgd)

Illustrations by Diana Kizlauskas

Photograph 20 Getty Images

ISBN 13: 978-0-328-39703-2
ISBN 10:   0-328-39703-2

Copyright © Pearson Education, Inc. or its affiliate(s). All Rights Reserved.
Printed in the United States of America. This publication is protected by copyright and permission should be obtained from the publisher prior to any prohibited reproduction, storage in a retrieval system, or transmission in any form or by any means, electronic, mechanical, photocopying, recording, or otherwise. For information regarding permission(s), write to: Pearson School Rights and Permissions, One Lake Street, Upper Saddle River, New Jersey 07458.

Pearson and Scott Foresman are trademarks, in the U.S. and/or other countries, of Pearson Education, Inc. or its affiliate(s).

1 2 3 4 5 6 7 8 9 10 V010 17 16 15 14 13 12 11 10 09 08

Selene lives in Chicago, Illinois, with her parents and her two younger sisters, Gwen and Corinna.

The family lives in a brick townhouse with planters in every window that grow bright red geraniums in the summertime. They have a kitten named Suki and two fat, lazy goldfish.

Selene loves to play soccer and invent games of make-believe with her little sisters. Sometimes they are explorers, digging in the closets for dinosaur bones. Other times they are master chefs at a fancy restaurant or astronauts on a new planet.

One December, school was out for winter break. Even though it was too cold to play soccer, Selene didn't have any trouble staying busy. She drew pictures, read books, and played with her sisters and her friends.

Selene has a special friend named Anneka. Anneka is Selene's pen pal from Stockholm, Sweden.

Sometimes Selene and Anneka exchange letters by mail, along with pictures or short stories they write for each other. Other times they send e-mails, which are much faster. It takes about a week for a letter to reach Sweden in the mail from Illinois, but only a minute to send an e-mail message.

Like Selene, Anneka has two younger siblings, and she loves to draw. She is also eight years old. She lives with her parents, her brother, Oskar, and her baby sister, Astrid. Anneka's family lives in an old farmhouse with a pond behind it. They keep goats and chickens. Anneka likes to skate on the pond in the winter.

Anneka looks forward to getting mail from Selene, who is far away in a country she has never visited. Selene's letters and drawings always make Anneka laugh. Selene's stories give her good ideas for make-believe games to play with her younger brother.

After lunch one day, Selene sent an e-mail to Anneka. She wrote about how Suki had tried to catch one of the goldfish and splashed water on the floor. She also wrote about the snowball fight she and her sisters had that morning. At the end of her e-mail, she added, "P.S. It's almost time for Kwanzaa!"

The next day, Selene eagerly read Anneka's reply. Anneka wrote about the book she had just finished reading and told a funny story about her baby sister. At the end of the email she wrote, "P.S. What is Kwanzaa?"

Selene found her father in the living room with Gwen and Corinna.

"Daddy, my friend Anneka doesn't know what Kwanzaa is," she said. "I want to tell her about it, but I'm not sure what to say. I know what we do on Kwanzaa, but I don't even know how it started."

"Kwanzaa started in the 1960s, when African Americans were fighting for their civil rights, which are freedoms that all people should have," Selene's father began. "An African American man named Maulana Karenga wanted to teach people about their history. Kwanzaa is a time to celebrate our African culture. It is a time for a special ceremony and for being with your family."

"What does the word *kwanzaa* mean?" asked Gwen, Selene's little sister.

Selene knew the answer. "*Kwanzaa* is a word from the Swahili language," she told Gwen. "It means 'the first fruits'."

Their father smiled. "I think you know more about Kwanzaa than you think."

Selene wrote a letter to Anneka. She explained that Kwanzaa starts on December 26, and it lasts for seven days.

Selene told Anneka her family would gather to honor their ancestors and their culture. They would decorate a Kwanzaa bush with homemade ornaments. They would set a table with an ear of corn for each child in the family. They would also set out a carved cup, or *kikombe*, for the grown-ups.

"Every night," Selene wrote, "we will light the *kinara*, which is a seven-holed candleholder. The candles are black, red, and green, and each one represents a different value, such as responsibility, faith, and creativity.

"On the last night of Kwanzaa, we will exchange homemade gifts and have a big feast. I can't wait!"

Selene finished her letter. Then she drew pictures for Anneka of all the Kwanzaa symbols she had talked about.

A week later, Selene got a reply from Anneka. It read:

Dear Selene,

Thank you for telling me about Kwanzaa. I wish I could see your family celebrating this holiday. The last night sounds like fun! Now I want to tell you about the holiday we are going to be celebrating soon called Luciadagen. It means Saint Lucia Day.

The festival of Saint Lucia is celebrated on December 13, which is one of the longest, coldest, and darkest nights of the winter in Sweden.

The story of Saint Lucia is that during the Middle Ages, a horrible famine happened in Sweden. People didn't have food to eat. Saint Lucia appeared dressed in white wearing a crown of lights on her head. She brought food to the hungry villagers.

My family honors Saint Lucia by lighting candles, eating special foods, and singing carols.

Early in the morning, the oldest daughter of the family (that's me!) goes to her parents' bedroom, wearing a crown and a white dress with a red belt. The crown is made from sprigs of lingonberry. This plant symbolizes new life during the cold winter.

My mom used to wear a crown with real candles when she was little! The candles in my crown work with batteries. When I go to my parents' room, I take them a special breakfast of *lussekatts*, which are buns with raisins in them.

　　Younger daughters follow Lucia, as her angel helpers. Younger brothers follow dressed as star boys. They wear white robes and pointed hats and carry star-topped wands. This will be the first Saint Lucia Day for my little sister, Astrid. She's too young to walk behind me, so she is going to wear a white dress and Oskar is going to carry her.

　　After the morning celebration I'll go to school. My classmates and I will choose one girl to play Lucia. The girl will wear her candle crown and hand out lussekatts and gingerbread to everyone. She will also lead the class in a special song called "Santa Lucia." Last year, my friend Dagmar got to play Lucia. I hope this year it will be me! At the end of the day, we will all go outside to watch a candlelight parade down the streets of Stockholm.

Selene thought that the festival of Saint Lucia sounded like fun. She thanked Anneka for teaching her about the holiday.

"I wish I could see you and your family celebrating Luciadagen!" she wrote.

The night before Saint Lucia Day, Selene's mother helped her and her sisters make gingerbread.

"It's too bad we don't have the recipe for lussekatts," said Selene. "Gingerbread cookies will have to do."

Selene, Gwen, and Corinna all found white dresses that they could wear and some thick red ribbon to tie around Selene's waist. They made a crown from cardboard and sprigs of pine needles. Their father found some battery-operated lights to attach to it.

The next morning, Selene woke up early. She got her younger sisters out of bed and brought them down to the kitchen to prepare a tray of gingerbread and coffee. The girls put on their dresses, and Gwen and Corinna helped fasten the crown in Selene's hair.

The girls walked up the stairs into their parents' room, waking them with cries of "Happy Saint Lucia Day!" Their parents laughed and rubbed their eyes. They sat up and took their breakfast trays.

"I like this tradition!" Selene's mother said, taking a bite of the gingerbread.

A week later it was time for Kwanzaa. Selene and her sisters decorated the house and the Kwanzaa bush with flowers made of red, green, and black paper. Each night after dinner, the family gathered in the living room to light a candle on the kinara.

On the last night of Kwanzaa, Selene gave her mother a jewelry box she had made and decorated with brightly colored beads. She gave her father five bookmarks that she had painted. She gave Gwen a little book she had written, and Corinna a paper doll she had made. After dinner the party began.

At the end of the evening, Selene's grandfather gave the final speech, and then they all went to bed.

That same day in Sweden, Anneka was wrapping some gifts she had made for her family. She made a walking stick for her father with his initials carved into the wood. She made her mother a painting of her favorite hen. She made Oskar a drum, and for Astrid, a mobile with bright blue ribbon and bells that jingled.

"Happy Kwanzaa!" she exclaimed, giving each of her family members a package.

"What is this?" asked her father, laughing.

As her family opened their gifts, Anneka explained about Kwanzaa.

"I think this is a great tradition," said her mother, hugging her tightly.

A few weeks later, Selene got a letter in the mail from Anneka. Anneka wrote that she had been chosen to play Lucia at school. She also wrote about celebrating the final day of Kwanzaa with her family. She included a picture of her family on Saint Lucia Day and on Kwanzaa.

Selene thought about holidays and celebrations. Although Kwanzaa and Saint Lucia Day are different, they are both about being with your family and remembering your history. Selene was happy that she and Anneka had taught each other so much. She felt lucky to have a friend from another country.

Selene went to her room and wrote a reply to Anneka. She told her about the gifts she had made her family members for Kwanzaa and about all the different foods at the party. She also told Anneka how much fun she had playing Saint Lucia and making the crown with her sisters. In the envelope she included a photograph of herself wearing the crown of pine needles. She also drew a picture of her and her sisters bringing their parents gingerbread and coffee. As she was addressing the letter, Selene's sister Gwen stuck her head in the door.

"Ask your friend Anneka to teach us about more Swedish holidays," said Gwen.

Cultural Celebrations

Almost all cultural groups have celebrations or festivals. Chinese New Year is celebrated in February with parades and fireworks. Families eat foods they hope will bring good luck: chicken for prosperity, a whole fish for togetherness, and long noodles for long life.

In Basel, Switzerland, people have celebrated *Fasnacht* since the Middle Ages. For this carnival, there is music and dancing, and people wear masks and fancy costumes.

People in Basel, Switzerland, celebrate Fasnacht.